# Stargaze

T0317896

## Contents

Written by Alison Milford

## Collins

# The stars

On a clear night, there can be hundreds of stars.

It can be fun to find stars and share stories about them.

# Setting up to stargaze

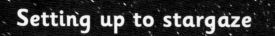

What to bring:

- chair
- **star map**
- torch

4

What to do:

- find a spot that's dark
- stare at the stars
- find some shapes in the stars

5

## What are stars?

Stars are balls of hot gases.
Their **glare** can be seen for
thousands of miles.

sun

# Where are stars?

The earth **rotates**. This means that the stars will be in different spots on different nights.

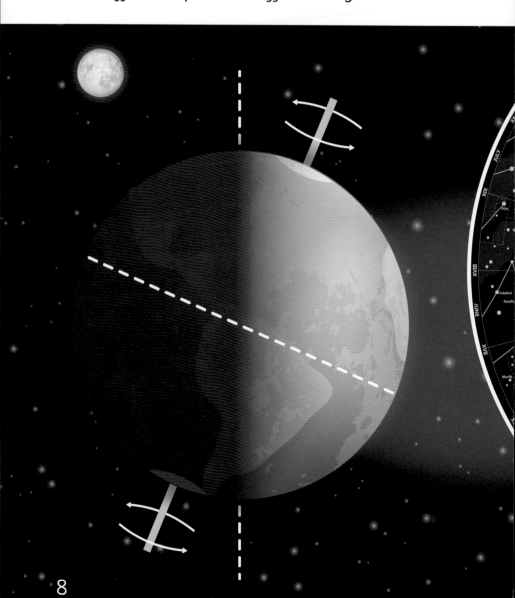

Star maps show us where they are.

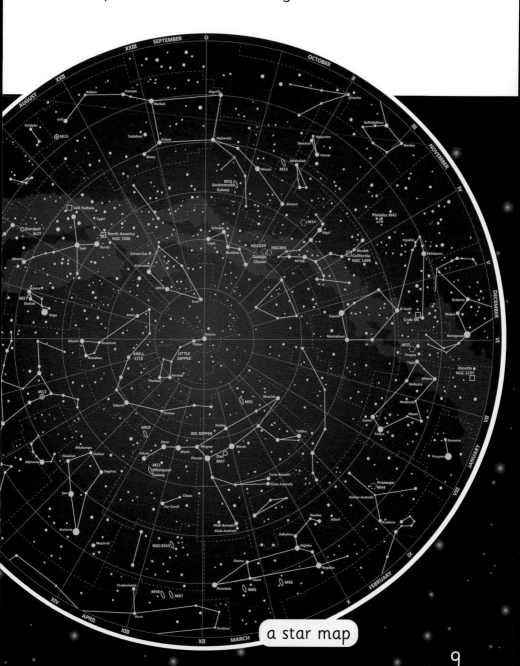

a star map

9

# Seeing star-shapes

Long ago, people discovered that groups of stars made shapes. They shared stories about them.

Here are some star-shapes.

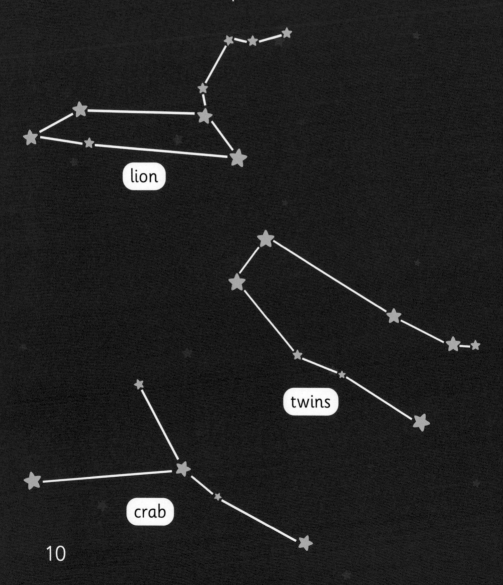

lion

twins

crab

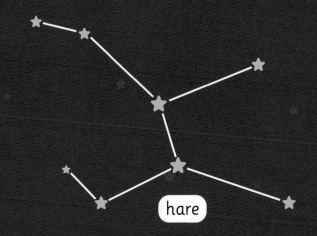

hare

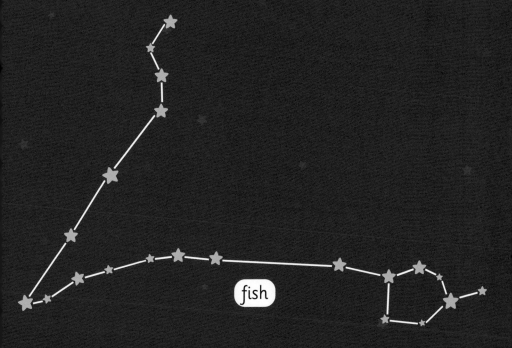

fish

# The Big Dipper

This star-shape is the Big Dipper.
It has a square cup.

square cup

The Big Dipper is part of the Great Bear.

Just look near the Big Dipper's cup.

North Star

Big Dipper

The North Star shows us where north is.

# Orion the hunter

To discover Orion, look for the three stars of his belt.

weapons

armour

belt

There is a red star near one of his arms.

# Brightest stars

Our brightest star is to the left of Orion's belt.
It is part of a dog-shape.

Orion

brightest star

Orion's biggest star is 70 times bigger than our sun!

# Myths

On clear nights, you might discover a band
of stars.

One **myth** says this band of stars is **embers** from a fire.

Another myth says it is spilt milk.

## Planet-spotting

You might see some **planets** among the stars when you stargaze.

You will need a **telescope** to see other planets.

Each planet has a colour.

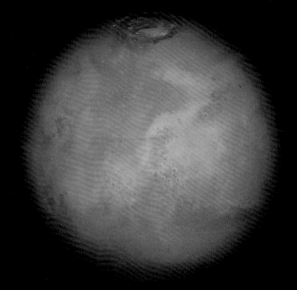

Mars looks red.

Jupiter looks brown.

Saturn looks yellow.

planet

Unlike stars, planets don't shimmer.

# Shooting stars

Shooting stars are not stars. They are small rocks that burn in the air over Earth.

No matter where you gaze, the night is full
of wonders!

# Glossary

**embers**  small bits of wood or coal from a fire that glow with heat

**glare**  bright light

**myth**  tale from long ago. Myths are not facts.

**planets**  big objects that go round a star

**rotates**  spins

**star map**  a map that shows where the stars are at a given time

**telescope**  an object that lets people see things far away

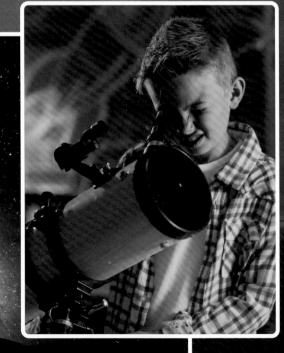

# Index

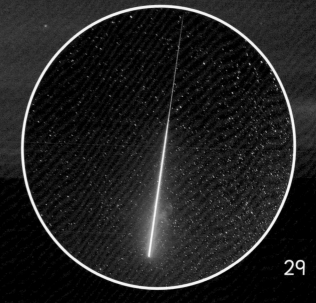

# Name the things

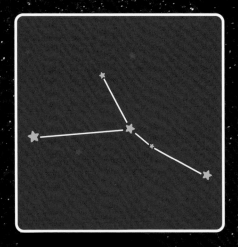

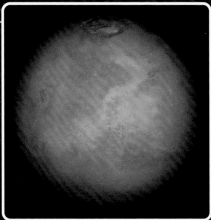

# After reading

**Letters and Sounds:** Phase 5

**Word count:** 357

**Focus phonemes:** /ai/ ay, a-e, ey /ee/ ie, ea /igh/ i-e, i /oa/ o, ow, o-e /oo/ ou /ow/ ou /or/ al /ur/ ear /e/ ea /i/ y /ear/ ere /air/ ere, ear, are /u/ o, our, o-e

**Common exception words:** of, to, the, full, are, be, do, when, what, where, says, our, their, people, one

**Curriculum links:** Science: Earth and space

**National Curriculum learning objectives:** Reading/word reading: read accurately by blending the sounds in words that contain the graphemes taught so far, especially recognising alternative sounds for graphemes, read accurately words of two or more syllables; Reading/comprehension (KS2): understand what they read, in books they can read independently, by checking that the text makes sense to them, discussing their understanding and explaining the meaning of words in context; identifying main ideas drawn from more than one paragraph and summarising these

## Developing fluency

- Take turns to read a page. Check that your child reads the labels and reads sentences with exclamation marks with expression.

## Phonic practice

- Focus on words that contain /air/ and /u/ sounds.
  - Ask your child to identify the spellings of /air/ sounds in the following words.

    where (*ere*)     square (*are*)     bear (*ear*)

  - Ask your child to read these words and identify the letters that make the /u/ sound.

    some (*o-e*)     other (*o*)     armour (*our*)     colour (*our*)

## Extending vocabulary

- Challenge your child to suggest a synonym for each of the following words.

  page 5: spot (e.g. *location, place*)     page 8: rotates (e.g. *spins, turns*)
  page 14: spot (e.g. *detect, make out*)     page 20: band (e.g. *line*)